Incandescent Leadership

Jessica R. Dreistadt

Incandescent Leadership

© 2013, 2016 Jessica R. Dreistadt.

All rights reserved. No part of this publication may be reproduced, distributed, or transmitted in any form or by any means, including photocopying, recording, or other electronic or mechanical methods, without the prior written permission of the publisher, except in the case of brief quotations embodied in critical reviews and certain other noncommercial uses permitted by copyright law. Requests for permission to use or reproduce material from this book should be directed to utopia@fruitioncoalition.com.

ISBN 978-1537727318

The Fruition Coalition
Lehigh Valley, PA
www.fruitioncoalition.com
www.jessicardreistadt.com

Table of Contents

Introduction	4
Purpose	7
Becoming	14
Connection	21
Compassion	28
Energy	35
Wisdom	42
Inspiration	49
Responsiveness	56
Creativity	63
Transformation	70
Incandescent Leadership Summary	77
Incandescent Reflections	78
Incandescent Intentions	79

Introduction

Incandescence has several general meanings. The first and most frequently used meaning is a **light that emerges from warmth**, such as incandescent lightbulbs. A similar definition is **brightness**. Incandescence can also be used to mean **clarity**. Another definition of incandescence is **passionately purposeful**.

Sounds like great leadership, doesn't it?

A few years ago when writing for my blog, The Activist's Muse, I differentiated between thinking of leaders as suns and thinking of them as nebulae. **Suns** are situated at the center of a galaxy. All of the planets revolve around the sun and are dependent on it for survival. Suns are established, static, and reliable. In contrast, **nebulae** are celestial clouds from which stars, planets, and other objects emerge. Nebulae are vulnerable, mysterious, open to possibility, and creative. Both are vital for our survival and advancement.

Incandescent Leadership blends these two concepts into a new understanding of leadership that **balances and integrates both paradigms**. In this model, suns and nebulae are not contradictory or in competition but rather are two very small components of a **greater whole**. Incandescent Leadership is a means to channel **positive universal energy** through **worldly thoughts and actions**. Just as incandescent lightbulbs mirror the sun's rays, we **become reflections of celestial suns and nebulae in our own little worlds**.

Incandescent Leadership is a **model of leadership**, but more importantly it is a **process of structured self-discovery** through which you can **identify and build upon your distinctive radiance and brilliance**. Each incandescent leader is a **unique cosmic being**.

Incandescent leaders share certain characteristics. We:

- are centered in our **purpose**;
- are continually awakening and **becoming**;
- feel a strong sense of **connection** to everything and everyone in the universe;
- glow with the warmth of **compassion**;
- generously share our abundant, renewable **energies** with others;
- illuminate **wisdom** and understanding;
- **inspire** others through gentle rays of light;
- fluidly **respond** to spontaneous movements;

- radiate **creative** brilliance; and
- create waves of **transformation**.

While incandescent lightbulbs are becoming a thing of the past, **Incandescent Leadership is on the rise**. This workbook will help you explore and articulate your own incandescence so you can **glow through your leadership**.

Our inquiry will investigate your leadership in each of the ten areas described on the previous page. To review, they are:

- purpose;
- becoming;
- connection;
- compassion;
- energy;
- wisdom;
- inspiration;
- responsiveness;
- creativity; and
- transformation.

Each section includes provocative questions to help you explore your incandescence. At the end of each section, there is a reflection page where you can record your overall impressions of, and ideas related to, the topic. After you explore and reflect upon each individual topic, you can begin **weaving together your discoveries** to create **individualized incandescent intentions** that will influence your leadership into the future.

You can work through this book from beginning to end, or select specific pages to ponder according to your proclivity. You might find it helpful to engage in this process with a friend or colleague, but you are free to do it on your own if that is your preference. There are **no right or wrong answers**. The questions are not a gauge to measure your incandescence; rather, they are a tool to uncover your own **unique feelings and ideas**. You have **unlimited time** to explore these pages. Hopefully, you will find this to be a fun, exciting **journey of self-discovery**!

I truly desire **enriched and enlivened leadership** for you, and I hope that the process of **reflecting, writing, and conversing** with others about the topics in this book leads you to that wondrous place. I would love to hear from you to learn about your Incandescent Leadership journey and to experience your incandescent approach to leading and living.

In celebration of your unique radiance and brilliance,

Jessica R. Dreistadt
Founding director, the Fruition Coalition

Purpose

Incandescent leaders are centered in our purpose. We:

- crave a life of **meaning**;
- are acutely aware of our **values and ideals**;
- declare our **intentions**;
- honor implicit agreements to consistently live with **integrity**; and
- are devoted to expressing courageous **passion**.

What does purpose mean to you?

Incandescent leaders crave a life of meaning. We are continually searching for deeper and more resonant ways to make sense of our lives. We aspire to make a profound impact rooted in our unique life purpose.

Why is your life meaningful?

What lenses, metaphors, stories, or ideas do you use to interpret the meaning of your life?

How does the meaning of your life connect with your leadership goals?

Incandescent leaders are acutely aware of our values and ideals. This awareness influences everything that we do. We seek higher and higher levels of integration in our leadership practice.

What do you value?

What are your ideals?

How do or will you intentionally integrate your values and ideals into your everyday leadership practice? How does this strengthen your leadership?

Incandescent leaders declare our intentions. We are in touch with our truest desires and make them known through prayer (if we have faith), conversation, and alignment with action.

What is it that you really, truly desire in your life?

How do or will you declare your life's intentions?

How does your leadership practice support the realization of your life desires?

Incandescent leaders honor implicit agreements to consistently live with integrity. We appreciate the gift of life that has been granted to us and recognize our responsibility to make the most of it by authentically integrating our purpose with our actions.

What does integrity mean to you?

How do you live with integrity?

How does your leadership practice reflect or not reflect your commitment to integrity?

Incandescent leaders are devoted to expressing courageous passion. Our deep sense of purpose compels us to boldly share our passionate thoughts and feelings with others.

What are you deeply passionate about?

How do you express your passions when you are leading?

What is the impact of sharing your passions?

Reflections on Purpose

In the space below, reflect on what you have learned about yourself and your leadership in this section.

Becoming

Incandescent leaders are continually awakening and becoming. We:

- are **vulnerable** and open to learning;
- cultivate and nurture the intricate gardens of **possibility**;
- **intensify and magnify** our core;
- engage in cycles of **renaissance**; and
- balance **acceptance and advancement**.

What does becoming mean to you?

Incandescent leaders are vulnerable and open to learning. We recognize that our leadership practice is a journey through which we continually learn and grow.

How are you vulnerable in your leadership practice?

How does vulnerability feel to you? How does this help or inhibit your leadership practice?

How does your leadership journey provoke learning and growth?

Incandescent leaders cultivate and nurture the intricate gardens of possibility. We are optimistic and hopeful, but practical and tactical in creating the beautiful world that we envision.

What possibilities is your leadership practice actively creating?

How do you cultivate and nurture these possibilities in your daily leadership practice?

How do you invite others to work and play in your garden of possibility?

Incandescent leaders intensify and magnify our core. As we grow and become more of who we truly are, our purpose is clarified and strengthened. It becomes more visible and impactful through higher levels of integration.

What is at the core of who you are?

How does this core become more clear and stronger through your leadership practice?

How do you make your core visible to others?

Incandescent leaders engage in cycles of renaissance. We have a fluid identity that is rooted in our purpose and values but open to re-interpretation. We let go of our old self-images in favor of those that more fully and accurately reflect who we truly are.

What is your identity as a leader?

How has your identity transformed over the years?

How does your self-image reflect or not reflect who you truly are as a human being?

Incandescent leaders balance acceptance and advancement. We unconditionally appreciate ourselves and others as we are at the moment but remain open to personal transformation and rebirth.

What do you appreciate about yourself? Others?

What do you not appreciate about yourself? Others?

How does or can unconditional appreciation influence your leader-ship practice and impact?

Reflections on Becoming

In the space below, reflect on what you have learned about yourself and your leadership in this section.

Connection

Incandescent leaders feel a strong sense of connection to every-thing and everyone in the universe. We:

- are curious about the **mysteries** of the universe;

- appreciate the delicate **complexities** of life;

- recognize that all of the particles in the cosmos are infinitely **inter-connected**;

- yield to the power of **trust and freedom**; and

- actively promote **mutuality and reciprocity**.

What does connection mean to you?

Incandescent leaders are curious about the mysteries of the universe. We resist the temptations of controlling and labeling and instead intentionally explore possibilities to discover deeper and broader levels of understanding about enigmatic ideas.

What puzzles you about the world? What do you know for sure?

How does your curious mind guide and influence your leadership?

How do you promote curiosity when collaboratively exploring problems and possibilities?

Incandescent leaders appreciate the delicate complexities of life. While clarity of understanding can be empowering and transformational, unjustified oversimplification can obscure great beauty and wonder. We want to comprehend, rather than conceal, complex details and relationships.

What complexities mystify you as a leader?

How do you seek greater understanding of these complexities?

What details do you conceal? What details are concealed to you? Is the purpose of concealment to clarify or to control?

Incandescent leaders recognize that all of the particles in the cosmos are infinitely interconnected. Each breath we take, every thought that floats through our mind, and all of the many things that we do, have a profound impact throughout the entire universe.

How are your thoughts, feelings, and actions connected to the cosmos?

How are all of the thoughts, feelings, and actions in the cosmos connected to you?

How can you heighten awareness of interconnectedness in your leadership?

Incandescent leaders yield to the power of trust and freedom. Controlling and constricting leads to suppression and distortion of our collective inherent freedoms. We courageously let go of anything that does not fully resonate with our values. We believe that we al-ready are everything that we need and everything that we desire.

Are you trusting? Who do you trust? Who do you not trust? Do you trust yourself? Are you trusted?

How do your actions create individual material and relational freedoms that reflect our collective spiritual and emotional freedoms?

What do you need to let go? What is stopping you from doing this? How does it feel to let go?

Can everything that you truly need or desire be found within your heart, mind, or spirit? Why or why not?

Incandescent leaders actively promote mutuality and reciprocity. We prefer to share rather than give and take. We expect no more from others than we are willing to share ourselves. We engage in supportive, egalitarian relationships.

What do you have to share? Do you freely share with others?

What do others have to share with you? Do you freely receive from others?

Do your relationships feel supportive and egalitarian? If not, how can you change this?

Reflections on Connection

In the space below, reflect on what you have learned about yourself and your leadership in this section.

Compassion

Incandescent leaders glow with the warmth of compassion. We:

- are **conscientious** about the impact we have on others;
- sincerely **empathize** with others;
- generously express **lovingkindness** toward ourselves and others;
- attempt to **accept and forgive** ourselves and others; and
- gracefully promote global **harmony**.

What does compassion mean to you?

Incandescent leaders are conscientious about the impact we have on others. We consider the ripple effects of everything we think, say, and do. We are aware of our ability to make a difference and use all of our power to support humanity and the planet.

How are you a conscientious leader?

How do your thoughts, words, and actions impact others?

What abilities and powers are accessible to you? How do you intentionally use these for the greater good?

Incandescent leaders sincerely empathize with others. We care about others' feelings and overall wellbeing. Our empathy is universal and unconditional.

When do you feel especially empathetic? When do you not feel empathetic?

How does empathy impact your leadership practice?

As a leader, how do or can you intentionally express your feelings of empathy? How can you promote a greater sense of universal empathy?

Incandescent leaders generously express lovingkindness toward ourselves and others. We consistently practice tender loving care. We openly and frequently share the goodness in our hearts with others.

How do you express lovingkindness toward yourself?

How do you express lovingkindness toward others?

How does or can lovingkindness influence your impact as a leader?

Incandescent leaders attempt to accept and forgive ourselves and others. We let go of our anger when we feel betrayed. Difficult experiences are opportunities for us to learn about our feelings, needs, and strengths.

Do you carry anger and shame around with you? Why? How does this impact your relationships? Your leadership practice?

What is your process for forgiving someone who acted in a way that led you to feel hurt?

How does your organization interpret and process anger and shame? Is this healthy and constructive? If not, what could be done differently?

Incandescent leaders gracefully promote global harmony. We bring people and ideas together to fulfill individual and collective desires and dreams. Our actions promote greater love, understanding, and unity throughout the planet.

How do you support the desires and dreams of your friends, family, and colleagues?

How do you intentionally connect people and/or ideas to promote harmonious transformation?

How does your leadership create or restrict global love, understand-ing, and unity?

Reflections on Compassion

In the space below, reflect on what you have learned about yourself and your leadership in this section.

Energy

Incandescent leaders generously share our abundant, renewable energies with others. We:

- recognize that **love, power, and enthusiasm** are infinite energies that multiply when they are shared;

- ground our interactions in **real optimism and hope**;

- are attuned to the power of **resonance**;

- promote the vital **flow** of positive energies; and

- remember to regularly **refresh and replenish** our renewable energies.

What does energy mean to you?

Incandescent leaders recognize that love, power, and enthusiasm are infinite energies that multiply when they are shared. We joyfully use these resources for the greater good and sincerely desire for others' positive energies to be increased through our interactions.

How do you define power? How do you use and share power as a leader? What is the impact of this?

How do you share love and enthusiasm in your leadership? What is the impact of this?

What other energies are infinite and multiplicative? How can this influence your relationships and your leadership?

Incandescent leaders ground our interactions in real optimism and hope. We recognize that struggle and strife feel very real and destructive, but also realize the creative and transformative potential of conflict. Our difficulties do not diminish the sense of possibility and wonder that motivates us to always express our highest values.

Do you focus on surviving or thriving in your leadership practice—or both? Why? How does this influence you and your impact?

How do or can you remain focused on your vision and goals despite daily difficulties?

How do your actions reflect a prevailing sense of hope and optimism?

Incandescent leaders are attuned to the power of resonance. When we consistently and authentically align our thoughts and actions with our values, passions, and life purpose, we can realize our deepest desires and dreams. We emanate what we choose to create.

How do your thoughts and actions reflect your values, passions, and life purpose?

How are your thoughts and actions out of sync with your values, passions, and life purpose?

What steps can you take to intentionally calibrate your current reality to reflect your desires and dreams? What will be the impact of doing this?

Incandescent leaders promote the vital flow of positive energies. We both remove energy blocks and gently push energy along as we en-counter it. We do not accept the illusion that it is possible to grasp or hoard positive energy. The more we share, the more we will all have.

As a leader, what energies do you want to flow?

How can you promote the flow of positive energy?

How will an increased flow of energy influence your ability to lead and the impact of your leadership?

Incandescent leaders remember to regularly refresh and replenish our renewable energies. If we are not fully aware and intentional, we may develop internal energy blocks over time. These blocks can be dissolved by regularly enhancing our awareness through meditation or prayer and by creating opportunities to connect with our passions and purpose.

How can you tell that you are starting to develop an energy block?

How do you feel when your positive energy is blocked?

How do you feel when your positive energy is abundant and freely flowing?

What regular practices do or will you use to refresh and replenish your renewable energies?

Reflections on Energy

In the space below, reflect on what you have learned about yourself and your leadership in this section.

Wisdom

Incandescent leaders illuminate wisdom and understanding. We:

- are **naïve ingénues** who have insatiable curiosity;

- recognize that **intuition, imagination, and intellect** are complementary and mutually reinforcing;

- are both captivated and liberated by enthralling **ideas**;

- are contemplative **observers** and active **explorers** of life; and

- seek greater **awareness and clarity**.

What does wisdom mean to you?

Incandescent leaders are naïve ingénues who have insatiable curiosity. As we discover and develop an understanding of ideas, we are provoked to continue our never-ending exploration of concepts and connections.

Do you see yourself as an expert or as a "naïve ingénue?"

What does it feel like to learn? Is it exhilarating? Exhausting?

What ideas provoke your curiosity?

How do or will you develop a thirst for learning within yourself? Within others?

Incandescent leaders recognize that intuition, imagination, and intellect are complementary and mutually reinforcing. Taken together, these approaches reveal deeper dimensions of understanding than any one alone.

As a leader, how do you use your intuition?

As a leader, how do you use your imagination?

As a leader, how do you use your intellect?

How do you intentionally integrate your intuition, imagination, and intellect in your leadership practice?

Incandescent leaders are both captivated and liberated by enthralling ideas. We find ourselves lost in books, interesting conversations, and deep thoughts. While mundane tasks may escape our attention when we are engaged with ideas, the impact of our actions is duly strengthened by immersion in our collective imaginations.

What ideas are enthralling to you?

How do you learn about these ideas?

How does engaging with ideas inhibit and/or enhance your leader-ship practice?

Incandescent leaders are contemplative observers and active explorers of life. Our deep sense of caring leads to awareness and attentiveness to both details and the big picture. Our ideas are shaped by both distant observations and immediate experiences.

How do you observe in your leadership practice?

How do you explore in your leadership practice?

How does awareness and attentiveness influence your leadership practice and impact?

How do you integrate your observations and your experiences in your leadership practice?

Incandescent leaders seek greater awareness and clarity. We are not satisfied with superficiality; rather, we prefer to reveal the true, uncluttered meaning and purpose of everything we encounter.

What does clarity mean to you?

Why is clarity important in the practice of leadership?

As a leader, how do you encourage clarity and discourage superficiality?

Reflections on Wisdom

In the space below, reflect on what you have learned about yourself and your leadership in this section.

Inspiration

Incandescent leaders inspire others through gentle rays of light. We:

- stir and expose our **inner muse**;
- share our divine **visions**;
- create **sparks** that intensify the light within others' hearts and minds;
- spontaneously share **joy and bliss**; and
- **encourage and motivate** ourselves and others.

What does inspiration mean to you?

Incandescent leaders stir and expose our inner muse. We are connected to, and lovingly nurture, a deep internal source of inspiration. We induce our muse to come out and play whenever we can.

How does your inner muse inspire you as a leader?

How do or will you nurture your muse?

How do or will you call upon your muse both on a regular basis and when you are in need of inspiration?

Incandescent leaders share our divine visions. We allow possibilities to flow through us. When a vision for the future emerges in our hearts and our minds, we engage others to make it a reality.

Why is vision important in your leadership?

How do or will you allow possibilities to flow through you?

How do or will you engage others in the work of making your vision a reality?

Incandescent leaders create sparks that intensify the light within others' hearts and minds. We actively seek out the light in others, and use our energy to reveal and strengthen it.

As a leader, how can you seek out the light in others? How will doing this strengthen your leadership and your organization?

What energetic sparks do or will you use to amplify others' light?

How do or will you allow others to amplify your light?

Incandescent leaders spontaneously share joy and bliss. We feel a deep sense of love and connection that naturally flows through in our interactions with others. We create happiness and cheer whenever possible.

How would you describe the love in your heart?

How do you share this love with others through your leadership?

As a leader, how do or will you create more happiness in the world?

Incandescent leaders encourage and motivate ourselves and others. We are both inspired and inspiring. We love to be helpful to others but also remember to take care of ourselves first.

What motivates you?

How do you learn about what motivates others?

As a leader, how do and will you encourage your coworkers and colleagues?

Reflections on Inspiration

In the space below, reflect on what you have learned about yourself and your leadership in this section.

Responsiveness

Incandescent leaders fluidly respond to spontaneous movements. We:

- are open to **adventure and whimsy**;
- fully immerse ourselves in **peaceful journeys**;
- are **open, flexible, and flowing**;
- gracefully make whispering **waves**; and
- orchestrate **sweet symphonies**.

What does responsiveness mean to you?

Incandescent leaders are open to adventure and whimsy. We love to have fun and don't take ourselves or life too seriously. We live in the moment and take advantage of opportunities as they arise.

How is your leadership an adventure?

How is your leadership fun?

How do you promote adventure and fun in your workplace?

In your leadership, how do you live in the moment?

Incandescent leaders fully immerse ourselves in peaceful journeys. We love to both freely explore and pursue set destinations. Along the way, we dance with mystery and sing to the harmony of opportunity. Journeys are means to fully explore both our inner and outer worlds.

What journeys have you embarked on as a leader?

What leadership journeys are in your future?

How are these journeys opportunities to learn about your inner and outer worlds?

Incandescent leaders are open, flexible, and flowing. We resist prescription and constriction. While we are able to make definitive decisions, we like to keep our options open. We are always ready to respond to emerging opportunities.

How do you balance decision making with openness to opportunity?

How do you recognize opportunities as they emerge?

How is your leadership strengthened by flexibility?

Incandescent leaders gracefully make whispering waves. We not only respond to our environment, we also influence that environment and create opportunities for others to respond to us. The waves we create contribute to a stronger undercurrent of love, hope, and peace.

As a leader, when do you make waves?

How do you make waves?

What is the immediate and long-term impact of the waves you make?

Incandescent leaders orchestrate sweet symphonies. We curate, cultivate, and coordinate people, ideas, and resources so that we are all singing the same beautiful song that we collaboratively created.

How do you curate and cultivate ideas and resources?

How do you promote collaboration?

What would it take to get to a place where everyone is singing the same song?

Reflections on Responsiveness

In the space below, reflect on what you have learned about yourself and your leadership in this section.

Creativity

Incandescent leaders radiate creative brilliance. We:

- approach our work with **artistry and soul**;
- glow with the **possibility of our ideals**;
- revel in **rebellion**;
- are **inventive, imaginative, and innovative**; and
- generate and emanate **vivacity**.

What does creativity mean to you?

Incandescent leaders approach our work with artistry and soul. We are intentional about the intricate details of our leadership. In articulating our vision, we write poems, sing arias, and paint landscapes. We eschew artificiality and authoritarian impositions of expectations.

Describe the art of your leadership.

How is your leadership a unique expression of you-ness?

How to you respond to the many threats to artful leadership?

Incandescent leaders glow with the possibility of our ideals. Our enthusiasm and passion is consistently evident and contagious. Our inner vision and determination to realize it is only strengthened by external challenges.

How do your ideals shine through you?

How do others recognize your passion and enthusiasm?

How do challenges strengthen your resolve?

Incandescent leaders revel in rebellion. We reject conformity. Our rebellion is intentional and is a reflection of the deeper meaning we seek in all of our life experiences.

How is your leadership rebellious?

When do you conform as a leader? How does this contribute or de-tract from your passion and purpose?

What is the impact of rebellion in your leadership?

Incandescent leaders are inventive, imaginative, and innovative. We love to play with and create new ideas, products, and services. We crave novelty. We love to think about things differently than most other people.

How does your creativity distinguish you as a leader?

How is your thinking different from others? How is it similar?

What do you love to create? How is this integrated into your leader-ship practice?

Incandescent leaders generate and emanate vivacity. Our creativity and originality is a great source of joy. It is a powerful energy that is evident in our auras. We naturally remind people what life is really all about.

How are you vivacious as a leader? How are you not vivacious?

What is the impact of being a vivacious leader?

What would a world without vivacious leadership look like? What would the world look like if everyone was a vivacious leader?

Reflections on Creativity

In the space below, reflect on what you have learned about yourself and your leadership in this section.

Transformation

Incandescent leaders create waves of transformation. We:

- express consistent **devotion** to our dreams;
- **expand and flower** in response to stress;
- recognize and liberate beautiful **butterflies**;
- provoke and promote evolutionary **progress**; and
- realize revolutionary **renewal**.

What does transformation mean to you?

Incandescent leaders express consistent devotion to our dreams. We don't do this by clinging to our ideas, but by making them real through dialogue and action. As we create our dreams, we integrate new possibilities that emerge from within or through relation-ships with others to make them even more beautiful and tangible.

How do you express devotion to your dreams?

How do you involve others in the realization of your dreams?

How do your dreams evolve?

Incandescent leaders expand and flower in response to stress. Challenges reveal our inner beauty and dignity. We cultivate fertile ground in our hearts that flourishes regardless of the elements.

How do you respond to stress?

What do or will you do to flourish regardless of the circumstances?

What do or will you do to use challenge as an opportunity to grow?

Incandescent leaders recognize and liberate beautiful butterflies. Our world is overflowing with beautiful butterflies trapped in co-coons. These butterflies reside both within us and within others. We continually seek them out and set them free.

How do you recognize trapped butterflies?

How do you set butterflies free?

What would the world look like if all of the trapped butterflies were set free?

Incandescent leaders provoke and promote evolutionary progress. We are always moving forward, building upon what we have learned in the past. When we get stuck, we arouse our passions and energies to loosen up.

How do you move things forward in your leadership?

How do you know when you have truly provoked progress?

What do you do when you feel stuck?

Incandescent leaders realize revolutionary renewal. We pursue peaceful revolution through transformation in our own hearts. Each revolution is an opportunity for rebirth and renewal.

How do or will you pursue revolutionary change?

Do you direct your transformational efforts inward, outward, or both? Why?

How do you know when you have realized a revolutionary transformation?

Reflections on Transformation

In the space below, reflect on what you have learned about yourself and your leadership in this section.

Incandescent Leadership

Purpose
Incandescent leaders are centered in our purpose. We:
- crave a life of meaning;
- are acutely aware of our values and ideals;
- declare our intentions;
- honor implicit agreements to consistently live with integrity; and
- are devoted to expressing courageous passion.

Becoming
Incandescent leaders are continually awakening and becoming. We:
- are vulnerable and open to learning
- cultivate and nurture the gardens of possibility
- intensify and magnify our core;
- engage in cycles of renaissance; and
- balance acceptance and advancement.

Connection
Incandescent leaders feel a strong sense of connection to every-thing and everyone in the universe. We:
- are curious about the mysteries of the universe;
- appreciate the delicate complexities of life;
- recognize that all of the particles in the cosmos are infinitely inter-connected;
- yield to the power of trust and freedom; and
- actively promote mutuality and reciprocity.

Compassion
Incandescent leaders glow with the warmth of compassion. We:
- are conscientious about the impact we have on others;
- sincerely empathize with others;
- generously express lovingkindness toward ourselves and others;
- attempt to accept and forgive ourselves and others; and
- gracefully promote global harmony.

Energy
Incandescent leaders generously share our abundant, renewable energies with others. We:
- recognize that love, power, and enthusiasm are infinite energies that multiply when they are shared;
- ground our interactions in real optimism and hope;
- are attuned to the power of resonance;
- promote the vital flow of positive energies; and
- remember to regularly refresh and replenish our renewable energies.

Wisdom
Incandescent leaders illuminate wisdom and understanding. We:
- are naïve ingénues who have insatiable curiosity;
- recognize that intuition, imagination, and intellect are complementary and mutually reinforcing;
- are both captivated and liberated by enthralling ideas;
- are contemplative observers and active explorers of life; and
- seek greater awareness and clarity.

Inspiration
Incandescent leaders inspire others through gentle rays of light. We:
- stir and expose our inner muse;
- share our divine visions;
- create sparks that intensify the light within others' hearts and minds;
- spontaneously share joy and bliss; and
- encourage and motivate ourselves and others.

Responsiveness
Incandescent leaders fluidly respond to spontaneous movements. We:
- are open to adventure and whimsy;
- fully immerse ourselves in peaceful journeys;
- are open, flexible, and flowing;
- gracefully make whispering waves; and
- orchestrate sweet symphonies.

Creativity
Incandescent leaders radiate creative brilliance. We:
- approach our work with artistry and soul;
- glow with the possibility of our ideals;
- revel in rebellion;
- are inventive, imaginative, and innovative; and
- generate and emanate vivacity.

Transformation
Incandescent leaders create waves of transformation. We:
- express consistent devotion to our dreams;
- expand and flower in response to stress;
- recognize and liberate beautiful butterflies;
- ·provoke and promote evolutionary progress; and
- realize revolutionary renewal.

Incandescent Reflections

Looking back on your journey through this workbook, reflect upon what you have learned and what you hope to do differently in the future.

Some things I have learned about myself:

Some things I have learned about my leadership:

Some things I plan to change or do differently as a result of this book:

Incandescent Intentions

Our intentions are influenced by our thoughts and feelings. In turn, our intentions influence our actions and leadership impact. In the space below, map the connections among your incandescent thoughts, feelings, intentions, actions, and impact.

My incandescent thoughts:

My incandescent feelings:

My incandescent intentions:

My incandescent actions:

My incandescent impact:

Notes

www.ingramcontent.com/pod-product-compliance
Lightning Source LLC
Chambersburg PA
CBHW080721190526
45169CB00006B/2470